160

Sarah and Paul
Make a Scrapbook

D0993375

Discover about
The Lord's Prayer

Derek Prime

Christian Focus Publications

illustrations
by
Janis Mennie

Published by

Christian Focus Publications Ltd

Tain   Houston
Ross-shire   Texas

© 1990 Derek Prime

ISBN 1 871676 35 5

CONTENTS

To Anna, Emily, Deborah, Andrew and Paul

1   The Lord's Prayer

Sarah and Paul MacDonald, who were twins, loved asking questions. Some of the questions they asked were very good ones. Most Sundays at church they prayed The Lord's Prayer. Like many boys and girls they knew it by heart, and sometimes Sarah and Paul prayed The Lord's Prayer at home too.

One day after they had prayed this prayer together, Sarah asked her father, 'Dad, why do we call that prayer The Lord's Prayer?'

'That's an easy question to answer, Sarah,' replied Mr MacDonald. 'It was the prayer the Lord Jesus taught to His disciples. The disciples used to watch the Lord Jesus praying. They saw how much prayer meant to Him and they wanted to pray like the Lord Jesus; but they didn't know how to do so.'

'I'd like to know too,' added Sarah.

'Well, one day, after they had watched Jesus pray again, they went to Him and said, "Lord, teach us to pray like You."'

Paul asked, 'But why do we have to say that prayer so often, Dad? Why did Jesus teach only one prayer?'

Mr MacDonald thought for a moment. 'So

that we would have a pattern or a model,' he said.

'I don't quite understand,' said Sarah. 'I know about knitting patterns. But can you have a prayer pattern?'

'Yes, you can. When Mum does her knitting she has a pattern which tells her how to make the thing she wants to knit. If it's a jumper, she wants to make, she has a jumper pattern; if it's a pair of socks, she buys a sock pattern. The prayer the Lord Jesus taught His disciples is a kind of pattern too. We can pray it ourselves, but it also tells us how to make our own prayers. It is a model prayer.'

'Model prayer! I'm interested in models,' said Paul. 'Only the other day Uncle Leslie showed me a model of some buildings he's helping to make.'

'Yes,' replied his father. 'Often, an architect will have a model made of the building he has planned before the building itself is started, so that people can see what it's going to be like. It helps the builders to see the model too. The Lord Jesus gave us The Lord's Prayer to show us how to build our own prayers.'

'Does that mean we should pray only this prayer to God?' asked Sarah.

'Oh, no,' said her father. 'We can use this prayer ourselves, and it's good for us to pray it together because it's the family prayer in which we say not "My Father" but "Our Father". But most of all The Lord's Prayer helps us to make our own prayers.'

'How does it do that, Dad?' asked Paul.

'It explains first of all how we should come to God,' replied Mr MacDonald. 'It tells us what we ought to call God when we speak to Him. It tells us too the kind of things we can ask Him for. There are some things it's quite silly to ask God for.'

'I think I know what you mean,' said Sarah. 'I asked for a new bicycle and I didn't get one. It wasn't really the right kind of prayer because I know I was being selfish.'

'Yes, we all pray selfishly sometimes, I'm afraid,' said Mr MacDonald 'and that's why the Lord Jesus gave us this model prayer to teach us to pray as God wants us to pray.'

'I do wish you would explain what the prayer really means then,' said Paul. 'I don't understand when it says, "Hallowed be Thy Name". And what's "temptation"?'

'Look. I know what we'll do. Every night at bedtime, before you say your own prayers, I'll

8

tell you about a small part of The Lord's Prayer.'

'That will be fine,' exclaimed Sarah.

'Wait a moment though,' added her father. 'I've another idea too. You know how at school you sometimes have a special project. Why don't you make a kind of scrapbook and write down every night the things we learn from The Lord's Prayer? Then perhaps you could make some drawings or paste in some pictures to help you remember what we say.'

'Can we start tonight?' asked Paul.

'Yes; I think you'll find two large notebooks in the centre drawer of my desk. You can use those instead of proper scrapbooks if you like.'

In a moment Sarah and Paul had found the notebooks. They were the kind they liked because they were spiral-bound, which made it easy to turn over the pages.

'What are you going to write down first?' asked Mr MacDonald. 'What have you learned tonight?'

'Well,' said Sarah, 'first of all, God wants us to talk to Him.'

'Yes, what else?'

'The Lord Jesus taught the disciples this prayer,' said Paul.

'Good. And what have you learned about

the prayer?'

'Oh,' Sarah said, 'it's a pattern prayer.'

'Yes, it's a model prayer,' said Paul.

Mr MacDonald was pleased that Sarah and Paul had remembered so much. 'I think you've enough to put down in your scrapbooks now, don't you?'

And so Sarah and Paul wrote these things in their books. They wrote three sentences:

'God wants us to talk to Him.'

'The Lord Jesus taught the disciples this prayer.'

'It is a pattern or a model prayer.'

While they were writing, Mr MacDonald said to the twins, 'Why don't you do a drawing to go with what you've put down? What could you draw this evening?'

'I think the best thing,' suggested Sarah, 'would be a picture of the disciples watching Jesus pray.'

'I'm going to draw the Lord Jesus standing up and the disciples coming to ask Him to teach them to pray,' said Paul.

2 The Best Father

Sarah and Paul were doing some sums. It wasn't school home-work, but the twins were going to have an arithmetic test at school and just for fun, they had been having a race to see who could do twelve sums first. Their mother had made them up for them. Mr MacDonald joined in to make it more of a competition. Much to the twins' amusement, he made a mistake: he forgot to carry ten when he was adding up. Paul and Sarah teased him for that.

'You aren't very good at sums!' joked Sarah. 'Imagine you getting one wrong.'

'Yes, I'm afraid I often make mistakes,' replied Mr MacDonald with a grin. 'It's what comes of always using a calculator.'

'I can think of another mistake you've made,' added Paul.

'What was that?' asked Mr MacDonald.

'You forgot to give us our pocket money this morning.'

'So I did,' replied Mr MacDonald, smiling. 'You don't really want it this week, do you?'

'We do!' shouted Sarah and Paul together.

'All right,' said their father as he put his hand in his inside jacket pocket to give them

their pocket money.

It was quite late now and Mrs MacDonald called out from the kitchen. 'Time for bed, you two. Clear away your things.'

'Oh,' exclaimed Sarah, 'don't forget that Dad promised to teach us more about The Lord's Prayer tonight. We must have that before we go to bed.'

'Just twenty minutes more then,' replied Mrs MacDonald from the kitchen. 'Don't waste any time. I expect Dad's ready to talk to you now.'

'I'm ready,' said Mr MacDonald. 'What's the first part of the prayer we are going to talk about?'

'Our Father which art in heaven,' replied Paul.

Sarah had a question right away. 'Can everyone pray this prayer, Dad?'

'Why do you ask that?' asked Mr MacDonald. 'Anyone can say the words.'

'No, I don't mean that,' said Sarah. 'Is it right for everyone to pray this prayer?'

'You can help to answer that question yourself,' replied Mr MacDonald. 'Did the Lord Jesus teach the prayer to everyone?'

'No,' replied Sarah, 'He taught it to the

disciples, not to everyone.'

'That's right,' said her father. 'It wasn't a prayer for everyone to pray, but for the disciples of the Lord Jesus. It's a very special prayer and that's why it begins "Our Father..." '

'Is God everyone's Father?' Paul asked.

'In a way He is, because He made everyone, so it's sometimes said that God is everyone's Father. But God tells us that He's only the Father of those who have been born into His family. Could your friend Kevin call me his father, Paul?'

'Of course not,' laughed Paul.

'Why not?'

'He wasn't born into your family.'

'Does your friend Linda belong to this family?' Mr MacDonald asked Sarah.

'No,' said Sarah, 'you know she doesn't.'

'Yes, of course, I do! But, you see, you can call someone your father only when you've been born or adopted into his family.'

'How do we become members of God's family then?' asked Sarah.

'I know the answer to that,' said Paul. 'It's when we believe that the Lord Jesus died on the Cross to save us from our sins and we ask Him to be our Saviour. God then forgives our sins and we become His children.'

'You're right,' said Mr MacDonald. 'When we believe on the Lord Jesus - as Paul has said - God sends the Holy Spirit to live in our hearts, and God calls that being born into His family. We become His children.'

'It's not easy to understand,' commented Sarah.

'Not at first,' agreed Mr MacDonald, 'and lots of people have felt the same. God's Spirit is the One who helps us to understand it.'

'Did Jesus talk about our becoming God's children?' asked Paul.

'Yes,' replied Mr MacDonald. 'One night the Lord Jesus was about to go to bed and there was a knock at His door. "Come in," He called out. And in came a man the Lord Jesus knew.'

'I know who it was,' said Sarah. 'It was Nicodemus.'

Mr MacDonald nodded. 'Nicodemus didn't understand at all how his sins could be forgiven and how he could have a home in heaven. The Lord Jesus explained it to him, as they talked together, "Nicodemus, what you need more than anything else is to become a member of God's family." '

'Did Nicodemus become a member of

15

God's family?' asked Sarah.

'I don't know for sure whether he did at that moment,' answered Mr MacDonald, 'but I think he did, because the Lord Jesus explained to Nicodemus what he had to do.'

'What did he have to do?' asked Sarah.

'Just as Paul said. Nicodemus had to believe on the Lord Jesus. If he did that, he became a member of God's family.'

'We sometimes talk about our fathers at school,' said Paul, 'and the things they do.'

'I hope you say some pleasant things about me,' joked Mr MacDonald smiling. 'But God is the very best Father, you can have. He never makes mistakes.'

'You do!' Sarah almost shouted. 'You made a mistake in those sums these evening.'

'Yes, but God doesn't make any mistakes and He never forgets anything.'

'You sometimes forget our pocket money as well,' Paul said with a laugh.

'Yes, I do,' admitted Mr MacDonald. 'But God never forgets; and He knows what's best for us. He never lets us down and He always takes care of us like a father.'

'We could call God our Maker or our King too, couldn't we, Dad?' asked Sarah.

16

'Yes, we could,' replied Mr MacDonald. 'But I am sure there's a very special reason why the Lord Jesus wants us to call God "our Father". God wants us to trust Him just as children do their father.'

Mrs MacDonald had finished her work and she came in to sit down while Mr MacDonald talked to Paul and Sarah.

'Yes, God wants us to come to Him - to know that we can trust Him, just as you trust Dad,' Mrs MacDonald added. 'You think of all the things you go to Dad for. Tell me some of them.'

'When we want some help with our jig-saw puzzles,' said Sarah.

'When we want our pocket money too,' added Paul.

'Sometimes we go to him because we want him to go out with us,' said Sarah.

'Yes, and sometimes we go to him just because we like being with him,' said Paul.

'They're good answers,' commented Mrs MacDonald. 'And each of them is true, in a way, about God. We pray to God because we want to be with Him. Just as you like talking to Dad when he comes home from work, so Christians like talking to God because He's their Father. We ask God, in our prayers, to be with us. And we can ask Him to help us when we've something difficult to do. We can tell Him the things we need.'

'But if God's in heaven,' asked Sarah, 'how does He know all that goes on here on earth? How does He know about me?'

'Although God is in heaven,' answered Mrs MacDonald, 'He can see everywhere and He is everywhere. Heaven is His special home, but there's nowhere that God doesn't see. You can pray to God wherever you are. But I think we've said enough for now.'

'May we put something in our scrapbooks?' asked Paul.

'What would you like to put in tonight?' Mrs MacDonald asked.

'I think,' said Sarah, 'it would be a good idea if we drew a picture of the Lord Jesus in His room with Nicodemus. And then, perhaps, like the comics, we could write in Jesus' words to Nicodemus.'

'What words shall we put in?' asked Paul.

'I'll put, "You need to be born into God's family," ' answered Sarah.

'What are you going to write underneath?' asked Mrs MacDonald. 'What have you learned?'

'If I were you, I'd write, "God is the Father of all who trust in the Lord Jesus," ' said Mr MacDonald. 'And, the second thing could be, "God is the best Father." '

3   Standing up for God

Paul and Sarah were waiting for their father to finish his dinner so that he could tell them more about The Lord's Prayer. They had their scrapbooks ready because they hoped there would be something interesting to draw after they had listened.

They were talking about school and some of the things that had happened that day.

'Did you see Old Simpson at lunch-time chasing the boys from the boiler-room?' Paul asked Sarah.

'Yes, I did,' she replied. 'He was very cross and I think he was going to tell Mrs Walters.'

Mr MacDonald was listening and he asked, 'And who is Old Simpson, may I ask?'

'He's the school janitor, Dad,' replied Paul.

'Then there was something wrong with the way you spoke about him, wasn't there?'

Sarah asked, 'You mean calling him "Old Simpson?" '

'Yes. You ought to be respectful to all people who are older than yourselves. "Mr Simpson" is how you should speak of him,' replied Mr MacDonald.

'I'm sorry, Dad,' said Paul, 'but everyone

calls him "Old Simpson." '

'But that shouldn't make any difference to you.'

'Paul had an argument which almost turned into a fight, today,' Sarah said.

Paul looked embarrassed.

'You're not telling tales, are you?' asked Mr MacDonald.

'No,' answered Sarah. 'I'm proud of Paul because the quarrel was all because of you!'

'How was that?' exclaimed Mr MacDonald with surprise.

'Well, Paul and David Temple were arguing about whose father is more important. David said his father is because he's an ambulance driver and Paul said you're more important because you're an engineer in charge of machines and engines. Paul stuck up for you very well, Dad.'

'That was good of you,' said Mr MacDonald, with a smile at Paul. 'But there was no need to argue over something like that. The world needs both ambulance drivers and engineers. I think we'd better change the subject before Paul's face goes any redder.'

'Yes, please,' pleaded Paul. 'Explain the next part of The Lord's Prayer, please, Dad. I don't understand what "Hallowed be Thy Name" means.'

'It's not as difficult as it sounds,' said Mr MacDonald. 'It means to respect and honour God's name. If you respect someone, you're very careful how you use his name. That's why I was cross with you for calling Mr Simpson "Old Simpson", because you weren't respecting him properly and you were speaking of him incorrectly. When we say, "Hallowed be Thy Name" we're praying that men and women everywhere might respect God and speak of Him properly.'

'Is that why swearing is wrong, Dad?' asked Sarah, because she had heard some men swearing, using God's Name wrongly, on her way home from school.

'Yes, it is,' replied Mr MacDonald. 'In this part of The Lord's Prayer we're asking God to make men and women ready to stand up for God's Name and not speak of Him in a way that's disrespectful.'

'Paul stood up for you at school, didn't he?' asked Sarah.

'Yes,' said Mr MacDonald, 'but instead of sticking up for ourselves we're praying that we might stand up for God's Name. Christians know that God's Name is more important than any other, because He alone is God. That's why we worship the Lord; and it's wrong to worship anyone else. When we go to church to worship God we're trying to show our respect for God and how much we honour Him. Can you think of any people in the Bible who stood up for God's Name by saying that it was right to worship only Him?'

There was a brief silence while Sarah and Paul thought.

'I know,' answered Paul, 'Shadrach, Meshach, and Abednego were told to bow down and worship a golden statue of King Nebuchadnezzar when they heard the sound of musical instruments. If they didn't, they would be thrown into a blazing furnace. But they knew that it was wrong to worship a statue or even a king and so they refused. The king threw them into the furnace but God kept them safe, and the king saw that he was wrong.'

'And there was the story of their friend Daniel too,' suggested Sarah. 'King Darius - I think it was - made a law that no one was to ask any god or man for anything except the king for thirty days. Daniel knew he must honour God and pray to Him every day. So he prayed just

the same - three times a day. When he was thrown to the lions, God sent an angel who shut the lions' mouths so they wouldn't hurt him.'

'Well done,' congratulated Mr MacDonald. 'Shadrach, Meshach, Abednego and Daniel all hallowed God's Name. They so respected and honoured God's Name that they wouldn't do or say anything to displease Him.'

Paul couldn't understand one thing. 'Why is God's Name to be respected? Shouldn't we want God to be respected more than His Name?'

'Yes, you're right,' replied Mr MacDonald, 'but really the two are almost the same. God's Name in the Bible stands for all God is. If I said to you, "Respect Mum," you'd know that I meant you to respect and honour her because of everything she means to us and because of all she does for us. When we pray for God's Name to be hallowed, we want people to remember all that God is and all He does for us. What kind of Person do you think of when you think of God?'

'I think of Him as being holy and loving,' answered Paul.

'And what has He done for us?'

'He made us,' answered Sarah. 'And then

He sent the Lord Jesus, His Son, to die on the Cross to save us from our sins.'

'Good,' replied Mr MacDonald. 'God's Name is "hallowed" when people understand these things and thank God for them. Any more questions?'

'One more,' added Sarah. 'Paul and I, and Mum and you, know what God's like and what He's done, and we thank Him. Why do we keep on praying this same prayer?'

'Well, we soon forget how good God is, don't we? And in this prayer we're asking God to help us always to remember how good He is, and to remember to respect and honour Him. We're also praying that people who don't care about God may come to respect and honour Him as we try to do.'

'What shall we write down in our books?' asked Paul.

'Three sentences, I think,' replied Mr MacDonald.

'God is holy and loving.'

'We should give Him honour and respect.'

'We should worship only God.'

'I'm going to draw Daniel in the lions' den,' said Sarah.

'My picture's going to be Shadrach,

Meshach and Abednego going into the blazing furnace,' Paul added.

4   The Greatest King

It was Wednesday evening. Every Wednesday Mr and Mrs MacDonald took it in turns to go to the midweek Bible study at church. This evening it was Mrs MacDonald's turn. Instead of the usual Bible study, it was a special missionary meeting.

'Who sends missionaries out to other countries, Dad?' asked Sarah.

'God does.'

'What do you mean?   Do they hear God's voice or something like that?'

'Not usually,' replied Mr MacDonald. 'First Christians may hear about people in other countries who've never heard of the Lord Jesus. Because the Bible says God wants everyone to hear about the Lord Jesus, they may feel that God wants them to go and tell the people. As time passes they become more and more sure that this is what God wants them to do. Then they know they would be wrong to stay at home.'

Paul came into the room then after bringing his scrapbook from upstairs for the next part of The Lord's Prayer.

'I've written, "Thy kingdom come" at the top of the page,' Paul said.

'Let's have a change this evening,' suggested Mr MacDonald. 'Instead of you asking me all the questions, let me begin by asking you one. Who rules over a kingdom?'

Sarah had the answer very quickly. 'A king or a queen.'

'As God has a kingdom then,' said Mr MacDonald, 'it means that God is a King. A king or a queen may rule over many parts of the world, but not over all the world. Our Father in heaven rules over everything. He's greater than all the kings and queens, presidents and rulers of the world put together.'

'But why do we pray, "Thy kingdom come?"' asked Paul.

'You know the answer to that already,' suggested Mr MacDonald. 'Can you remember what Jesus said to Nicodemus when he came to Him one night?'

'Yes,' replied Sarah. 'I wrote it in my scrapbook. "Jesus said, 'You need to be born into God's family."'

'Well done,' said Mr MacDonald. 'Now the Lord Jesus said a little more than that. He explained to Nicodemus, "If you want to enter God's kingdom, you need to be born into God's family". You see, there are two kingdoms on

earth - the kingdom of God and the kingdom of Satan. When we're born into this world we're born into Satan's kingdom. The Lord Jesus came to rescue us from Satan.'

'Is that why He died on the Cross, Dad?'

'Yes, Paul. When He died on the Cross, the Lord Jesus defeated Satan so that when we trust in the Lord Jesus, Satan has to let us go and we belong instead to God's kingdom. It's quite different from every other kingdom because people from all the countries of the world belong to it, whatever their colour or language.'

'You still haven't told us why we should pray, "Thy kingdom come" though, Dad,' said Paul.

'I'm just coming to that!' said Mr MacDonald, with a smile. 'God wants His kingdom to grow. He wants people everywhere to hear about the Lord Jesus.'

'That's why Mum has gone to the missionary meeting, isn't it?' asked Sarah.

'Yes,' said Mr MacDonald. 'The Lord Jesus said that His kingdom would grow bigger and bigger. Do you remember Grand-dad planting a peach stone in his garden and how you watched the tree grow? The Lord Jesus said His kingdom would grow like a tree.

What does Mum use yeast for?'

'When she makes bread or rolls sometimes,' said Sarah. 'It spreads through the dough and makes it rise nicely.'

'The Lord Jesus explained that His kingdom would spread throughout the world, just like yeast through dough. When we pray, "Thy kingdom come" we're asking God to help missionaries and preachers and Christians everywhere to work hard in telling people about the Lord Jesus so that God's kingdom here on earth will grow.'

'Shall we ever see it?' asked Paul.

'Yes, if we belong to it. When the Lord Jesus comes back, the time will have come for all Christians to see God's kingdom. When we pray, "Thy kingdom come" we're telling God we want that great day to come soon. The disciples were very upset when Jesus told them He was going to leave them. But He told them not to worry.'

'Why did He say that?'

'Well, Sarah, He told them not to worry because in His Father's kingdom there's lots of room. He said, "I'm going there on purpose to prepare a place for you. When everything is ready, I'll come and get you and then you'll always be with Me where I am." '

'What will it be like?' asked Paul.

'Very wonderful,' Mr MacDonald said. 'Can you imagine what it must be like to discover hidden treasure in a field?'

'Exciting!' exclaimed Paul and Sarah together.

'The Lord Jesus told the disciples that the kingdom of God is as wonderful as that. There will be no more sorrow and suffering. People won't be ill there. And most wonderful of all, we'll see the Lord Jesus.'

'Why doesn't it all happen now?'

'I can't completely answer that question, Sarah. But the Bible tells us that before all this happens, the message of the Lord Jesus has to be preached throughout the whole world. That's why we pray, "Thy kingdom come." '

'What shall we write in our books, Dad?' asked Sarah.

'God is the greatest King.'

'His kingdom grows when people trust in the Lord Jesus.'

'We shall see it when Jesus comes back again.'

'What are you going to draw in your books?'

Sarah couldn't quite make up her mind. 'I think I'll draw either a large tree growing in a garden or a picture of Mum making her dough for the bread.'

'I'm going to draw a man digging up treasure,' said Paul.

5   Pleasing our Father

Sarah was doing a jigsaw puzzle and Paul was reading a book about railways. Mr MacDonald had come home late that evening and had only just finished his dinner. Soon it would be bedtime for Sarah and Paul, but before that they wanted to hear more about The Lord's Prayer.

Mr MacDonald sat down in his armchair. 'Do you know what would really please me this evening?' he asked.

Sarah looked up first. 'What, Dad?'

'If one of you ran upstairs and fetched my slippers for me!' answered Mr MacDonald.

'Oh, Dad!' exclaimed Sarah. 'I do want to finish this jigsaw. There are only a few more pieces to do. I haven't time.'

'Doesn't either of my children love me?' asked Mr MacDonald with a pretended groan.

Like a shot Paul answered, 'Yes, of course. I'll get them.'

'No, I will,' shouted Sarah, a little ashamed of herself. Then in a great rush they both hurried upstairs to get the slippers, and soon they came down with one slipper each!

'Thank you,' said Mr MacDonald. 'It's

good to have such helpful children! Now the next part of the prayer for us to think about is "Thy will be done in earth as it is in heaven". What do you think those words tell us about heaven, Sarah?'

'I suppose it tells us that in heaven what God wants is always done,' she replied.

'Yes,' said Mr MacDonald. 'Heaven is the special home of God, and one of the things which makes it very special is that everyone who lives there wants to please God and always does what He wants. Here very few people want to please God and those who do try to please God often fail to do so.'

'The Lord Jesus pleased God when He lived on earth, didn't He?' asked Paul.

'Yes, He did, and He lived a perfect life,' replied Mr MacDonald. 'That's why He could teach this prayer. It wasn't always easy for the Lord Jesus to please His Father because it meant in the end dying on the Cross.'

'How do we know it wasn't always easy?' Paul asked thoughtfully.

'Well,' said Mr MacDonald, 'just before He was arrested and crucified, He went into a garden with His disciples. He said to them, "Sit down while I go and pray". Then He took with

Him Peter, John and James and began to be terribly upset. "My heart's nearly breaking", He told them. "Stay here with Me." '

'What happened then?' Sarah asked.

'He walked on a little way and fell down on His knees as He thought of how dreadful it was going to be to die on the Cross and bear the punishment for men's sin.'

'But that was why He had come into the world, wasn't it?'

'Yes, Paul. The Lord Jesus knew that His death on the Cross for our sins was His Father's will. So He prayed a wonderful prayer: "Thy will, not mine, be done". When we pray, "Thy will be done on earth as it is in heaven", we're asking God that we may be like the Lord Jesus - always putting what God wants before what we want. Can you tell me, Paul, how we can know what God wants to happen in the world?'

'That's easy,' answered Paul, 'you've told us before. God has given us the Bible, His Word, to show us what He wants. It's like you telling us this evening how we could please you; God tells us in His Book the things we can do to please Him.'

'Can you tell me any things you know God wants to happen?' asked Mr MacDonald.

'He wants us to give food to hungry people like refugees,' said Sarah. 'And He wants all the world to know the good news about Jesus.'

'And He wants us to be like the Lord Jesus,' said Paul, 'by doing the right thing and caring for people.'

'You seem to understand that well,' commented Mr MacDonald. 'When we pray, "Thy will be done in earth as it is in heaven", we're praying that all things - feeding refugees, telling people about the Lord Jesus and everything else we know that pleases God - should be done just as God wants them to be done. And this prayer teaches us too that we should ask God to help people to do these things. But there's something more important than praying, "Thy will be done in earth as it is in heaven". Can you guess what it is?'

Sarah and Paul thought for a moment, but they couldn't guess.

'It's to do God's will. There's little use asking God for His will to be done and then doing nothing about it.'

'The Lord Jesus told a story about a man with two sons which teaches us that,' said Mrs MacDonald who had come into the room and had been listening.

'Do you mean the story about the prodigal son and his brother?' Sarah asked.

'No,' continued Mrs MacDonald, 'it was another story. A man with two sons went to the first son and said, "Go and work in my vineyard today, my son". He said, "I won't". But afterwards he changed his mind and went. Then the father said to the other son the same thing and he said, "All right, father" - but he never went. Which of these two did what their father wanted?'

'The first one,' Sarah and Paul answered. Sarah added, 'I was rather like that first son when Dad asked me to get his slippers.'

Mr MacDonald smiled. 'God wants us not only to pray for His will to be done, but He also wants us to do what He wants. This is how we can show our love for Him. You show your love to Mum and me by trying to do things to please us and by doing as you're told. That's the way we can show our love to God too.'

'What shall we write down in our books?' asked Sarah.

Mr MacDonald thought for a moment and said:

'God wants us to please Him.'
'The Bible tells us what God wants.'

'We must try to do what God wants, to help answer our prayers.'

'And what are you going to draw?' Mrs MacDonald asked.

'I think I'll draw the two sons - one going off to do what he wanted, and the other going to work in the vineyard,' replied Paul.

'I'm going to draw the Lord Jesus praying in the garden, with the three disciples watching Him,' added Sarah.

6 Cream Cakes and Doughnuts

As it was Friday night and Sarah and Paul didn't have to go to school the next day, they were allowed to stay up to have a late snack with their mother and father. Somehow that Friday night snack seemed to taste better than anything during the rest of the week. Paul had obviously enjoyed his very much and his mother said jokingly, 'I don't think I'll need to wash your plate, Paul. It looks as clean as when I took it out of the cupboard!'

Sarah and Mr MacDonald laughed as Paul very carefully finished his last mouthful. 'It's all very well laughing now about eating,' said Sarah, 'but we didn't laugh very much at lunch time at school today. Mrs Templeton, one of the teachers of the top classes, saw that a lot of us had left some of our lunch. Joy Hillman had left most of hers, and Mrs Templeton said it was dreadful to waste so much food when there are hungry people in the world who would love to have just a quarter of what we eat every day.'

'Mrs Templeton was quite right,' agreed Mrs MacDonald. 'We ought to be very grateful for our food. Isn't "Give us this day our daily bread" the part of The Lord's Prayer Dad's

going to talk to you about this evening?'

'Yes, it is,' answered Paul.

'Well then,' said Mrs MacDonald, 'let's hear about it now while we're all sitting together at the table. We'll leave the dishes until afterward.'

'All right,' said Mr MacDonald. 'Have you any questions about the words "Give us this day our daily bread"?'

'Why do you only pray, "Give us this day our daily bread"? We want more than just bread, don't we?' asked Paul.

'Trust you to think of your stomach!' answered Mr MacDonald. 'Yes, we do need more than bread, but bread stands for all we eat and everything our bodies need, because bread is the most basic thing that we eat.'

'Does God really give it to us?' asked Sarah. 'Mum buys the bread in the shop, and she has to buy nearly all the other things we eat as well.'

'That's true, of course,' answered Mr MacDonald. 'But unless God gave us these things in the first place we wouldn't be able to buy them. It was God who made the wheat and who sent the rain and the sun to make it grow so that the baker has the flour he needs to make the bread.'

'Yes,' said Paul, 'but it's your money you use to buy it, isn't it?'

'Yes,' agreed Mr MacDonald, 'but if God hadn't given me a healthy body so that I could go to work, I couldn't earn money to buy the bread. So whether or not I buy it with money, it's God who gives me my daily bread. When I pray, "Give us this day our daily bread", I'm asking God to give me the health and strength to earn money by working, so that I'm able to look after you all, and to give you bread, and everything else you need.'

'I hadn't thought of that,' said Sarah.

'It's because God is the One who provides us with our food that we try to remember to thank Him every time we have a meal,' added Mrs MacDonald. 'That's why it was so wrong to waste food at lunchtime.'

'Is God really interested in what we eat?' asked Paul, because he remembered how great God is.

'Yes, He is,' replied Mr MacDonald. 'He wants us to have enough. The disciples weren't very worried about all the people who had listened the whole day to the Lord Jesus, but He knew they hadn't eaten and He wanted to give them something to eat. Do you remember?'

'You mean when Jesus fed the five thousand?' asked Sarah. 'When Jesus used the five barley loaves and the two fishes of the boy who had come to listen to Jesus.'

'Yes,' said Mr MacDonald. 'The Lord Jesus taught that God cares about our bodies and He's sorry for the hungry and wants to help them.'

Sarah didn't like bread and butter as much as Paul, and she asked, 'Would it be wrong to ask God for whipped cream cakes and doughnuts?'

Mr and Mrs MacDonald laughed. Mr MacDonald answered, 'It wouldn't be wrong really. But God doesn't want us to ask for more than we need, although He often gives us more. He wants everyone to have enough. He certainly doesn't mind us having cream cakes and doughnuts! But He wants us to think of others before thinking of things we don't really need. That's why we pray for others at the same time as we pray for ourselves. Try to think of the hungry children in the world when you pray this part of The Lord's Prayer.'

'That's a good idea,' said Paul. 'I must try to remember that. One last question, if Sarah hasn't got one. Why do we say daily bread?'

'The answer's simple really,' replied Mr MacDonald. 'When we don't trust God as we should we soon worry about what's going to happen in the future. God doesn't want us to worry about tomorrow or about next week; He just wants us to trust Him each day as it comes.'

'How do you know that, Dad?' Paul asked.

'Well, the Lord Jesus spoke about this. He said, "Don't worry about food and drink to keep you alive and about clothes to cover your body. Look at the birds; they don't sow and reap and store in barns, yet your heavenly Father feeds them. You're worth more than the birds! And why be worried about clothes? Look at the flowers; they don't have to work, yet God takes care of them. If God takes care of the birds and the flowers He will certainly take care of you, if you will trust Him." '

'I remember reading that in Sunday School,' Sarah said.

'When we pray, "Give us this day our daily bread", we're telling God we want to trust Him for each day. Now I think Mum can suggest some sentences for you to write down in your scrapbooks.'

'Yes, all right,' said Mrs Macdonald, 'and why don't you both see if you can find a picture of a loaf of bread, or some other food, among the adverts in the magazines in the rack? Then you could each cut one out and paste it in your books. If you can't find one, draw a loaf and draw the Lord Jesus taking the loaves and fishes from the boy. Underneath write:

"God's creation provides us with food.
God cares about our bodies.
God wants us to trust Him for everything."'

7   Saying Sorry

Paul MacDonald was in a bad mood.   He always enjoyed Saturdays, but this Saturday he had lost his pen, one that he had been given as a birthday present.   He thought he must have lost it when he went out to buy a plastic model construction kit, but when he went back to the shop he hadn't been able to find it.   And, besides this, he had broken an important part of the plastic model he was making, and the whole thing was ruined without it.   Paul was cross with himself and felt cross about everything.

At dinner-time Mr MacDonald was still cleaning the car, so Mrs MacDonald, Paul and Sarah went ahead and had their meal.   The evening before they'd had some gingerbread, one of their favourite cakes, but Sarah hadn't had her piece.   Mrs MacDonald had promised she would keep it for her and put it out for dinner today.   But when the time came for dessert Paul took it when Sarah wasn't looking and began to eat it.

Suddenly Sarah said, 'That's mine, Paul. Mum saved it from yesterday; you had yours then.'

'It's very selfish of you,' remarked Mrs MacDonald, and Paul began to look even more cross and sulky.

'I don't mind then,' said Sarah, 'I'll have something else instead.'

When dinner was cleared away, Mrs MacDonald said, 'Go and get your scrapbooks, please. And I should look a little happier if I were you, Paul, before your father comes in.'

Not many minutes after they had gone upstairs to get their scrapbooks, Mrs MacDonald heard loud voices squabbling. 'What's wrong?' she called up the stairs.

Paul replied in a very cross voice, 'Sarah has some of my coloured pencils and she used them last night without telling me.'

'I've said I'm sorry, Mum,' Sarah shouted down.

'That's all very well,' said Paul. 'But they all need sharpening again. I won't forgive you!'

'Paul,' said Mrs MacDonald, 'you've a lesson to learn. What part of The Lord's Prayer are we going to talk about this evening?'

Paul thought for a moment. ' "Forgive us our trespasses; as we forgive them that trespass against us." '

'Do you know what "trespass" means?' Mrs

MacDonald asked.

'No; not really,' Paul replied. 'I remember we saw a sign once on a farm gate saying, "Trespassers will be prosecuted". Dad said it meant that the law gave the farmer the right to stop people going into his field. If anyone went into it without his permission he was breaking the law and could get into trouble.'

'Well, then,' said Mrs MacDonald, 'to trespass is to do wrong to others, or to break a law. So in The Lord's Prayer we are praying, "Forgive us when we do wrong to You, Father, as we forgive those who do wrong to us." Now you, Paul, cannot pray that prayer and mean it at this moment. God will forgive our sins, and we must be willing to forgive others.'

'Oh!' exclaimed Paul. 'That means that if I don't forgive Sarah, I can't expect God to forgive me.'

'The Lord Jesus told a story to teach that,' said Mrs MacDonald. 'He said that there was once a king who decided to make his servants pay all they owed him. A man was brought to him who owed him millions. Since he had no means of paying, the master ordered him to be sold as a slave, together with his wife and children and all his belongings. When the man heard this, he fell at his master's feet. "Oh, be patient with me!" he cried, "and I'll pay you back everything I owe you!" The master was so sorry for him that he let the man go, and rubbed out all the debt.'

'That was kind,' said Paul.

'Yes, but that wasn't the end of the story. When this same man left his master, he found one of his fellow servants who happened to owe him just a little money. He grabbed him, seized him by the throat and said, "Pay me what you owe me." The man fell down at his feet and begged him, "Be patient with me, and I'll pay you." But he refused and went out and had him put into prison until he paid the debt.'

'That was a dreadful thing to do,' said Sarah. 'What happened then?'

'Well, the other servants were very upset when they saw what had happened and they went and told their master all about it. Then the master sent for the man.'

'I hope he told him off,' Paul said.

'He did more than that. "You wicked man," he said. "Didn't I rub out all that debt when you begged me to do so? Oughtn't you to have shown pity to your fellow servant just as I, your master, showed to you?" And the master was so angry that he handed him over to the prison until he paid back all he owed. When the Lord Jesus had finished the story, He said, "And that is how my heavenly Father will deal with you, unless you forgive one another from your heart." '

Paul knew now that he had been wrong to be cross with Sarah. But he had a question he wanted to ask. 'But God doesn't forgive me only because I forgive others, does He? Didn't Jesus die so that we could be forgiven? We sing that in the hymn, "There is a green hill far away' - 'He died that we might be forgiven ..." '

'Yes, you're right,' agreed Mrs MacDonald. 'But we can be forgiven through the Lord Jesus only when we're truly sorry about our sins and want to stop sinning - the Bible calls this "repentance" - and when we're really sorry about our sins we know that we must forgive others. We still sin, unfortunately, even when the Lord Jesus is our Saviour and we need God to forgive us every day. And when we really understand and appreciate God's forgiveness, we're happy and quick to forgive others.'

'But suppose Sarah kept on using my pencils, should I still have to go on forgiving her?' asked Paul. 'Should I forgive her two or three times?'

Mrs MacDonald smiled and said, 'The Lord Jesus' disciple Peter asked a question like that. He said to the Lord Jesus, "Master, how often must I forgive my brother when he does something wrong to me? Would seven times be enough?" '

'What did Jesus say?' Sarah and Paul asked together.

'He said, "No. Not seven times, but seventy times seven". Now how many times is that?' asked Mrs MacDonald.

Paul worked it out first. 'Seven sevens are forty-nine, then add a nought: that makes four hundred and ninety.'

'Phew,' said Sarah. 'I would lose count long before then and wouldn't know when to stop forgiving.'

'That's what the Lord Jesus meant,' added Mrs MacDonald. 'Don't keep count of how many times someone has wronged you; just keep on forgiving. If you remember how much God has forgiven you and that the Lord Jesus died so that you could be forgiven, I think you'll find it easier to forgive others.'

Paul understood it now. 'I'm sorry I got so

cross,' he said to Sarah.

'I'm sorry I used your pencils without asking you,' answered Sarah.

'Good,' said Mrs MacDonald. 'Don't you both feel happier now? When you forgive one another like that, you can pray this prayer and God will forgive you the things you've done which haven't pleased Him. Well, I've saved Dad a job this evening by talking to you about The Lord's Prayer.'

'Dad won't mind,' Sarah said.

'Why don't you surprise him and do your scrapbooks now,' suggested Mrs MacDonald, 'so that you can show them to him when he comes in. Draw a picture of that bad servant seizing his fellow servant by the throat. Over it you could put -

"Not 1x7
 but 70x7"

And underneath write -

"Only God can forgive sins."

"Our sins can be forgiven because the Lord Jesus died for sinners."

"We must forgive others when they do wrong to us." '

8   Temptation

Before Paul and Sarah went to bed on Sunday evenings Mr MacDonald usually had some fun asking them questions - a sort of quiz. They liked playing "True or False".   Mr MacDonald would tell them something about a person in the Bible, and they would have to say whether it was true or false.

'Abel killed Cain.   True or false, Sarah?'

'False,' replied Sarah quickly.

'The Lord Jesus met Paul on the Damascus road.   True or false, Paul?'

'True,' answered Paul.

'Now let me ask you a question about the talk we heard in church this morning,' suggested Mr MacDonald.   He did this to see whether Sarah and Paul had been listening.   'What did Mr Hill speak about?'

Sarah and Paul remembered what their minister had spoken on.   "Honesty," they both said together.

'But it's not always easy to be honest, is it, Dad?'

'What do you mean?' asked Mr MacDonald.

'Well, when I bought a magazine the other

day and counted my change on the way home, I discovered that I'd been given too much. I was tempted to keep it, but I knew that was wrong and I went back and explained the mistake. They were surprised that I had gone back, I think.'

Paul felt the same. 'I find it difficult at school. When a lot of us have misbehaved and Mrs Fox asks one of us what's been happening, it's very easy to tell a lie so that no one gets into trouble.'

'What you say is true,' said Mr MacDonald. 'It's sometimes hard to be honest. Many times, and sometimes suddenly, we'll find ourselves tempted to be dishonest.'

Paul nodded and said, 'I remember the time Mum bought two dusters at a sale. When we arrived home we found the man in the shop had given Mum three instead of two. Sarah and I were pleased, but Mum explained that was wrong and she asked us to take the extra duster back to the shop for her.'

Mr MacDonald nodded. 'That kind of thing often happens. The next part of The Lord's Prayer is "Lead us not into temptation, but deliver us from evil". Temptation is when we feel like doing something even when we know that it would be wrong.'

'Like thinking you may as well ride on a bus for nothing if the conductor doesn't ask you for your fare?' asked Sarah.

'Or thinking it would be nice to pick apples off other people's trees when they're not looking?' asked Paul.

'Yes,' agreed Mr MacDonald. 'Some temptations come to us when we're on our own - like riding on a bus. Do you remember the story in the Bible of the fall of Jericho?'

Sarah and Paul nodded.

'When Joshua and his men captured the city, Joshua told them they were not to take any of the people's possessions. But a man called Achan was tempted to take something. He saw a beautiful coat which he longed to have. And then he saw a lot of silver and gold. And so he took some of these things and hid them in his tent. He thought no one knew.'

'But God knew, didn't He?'

'Yes, Sarah. We may be tempted without anyone knowing about it, except God. Sometimes temptation comes to us when we're with others. Most boys wouldn't steal apples on their own, but if they're together, and one of them says, "Let's steal some apples," they may all do so because no one wants to be thought of as a coward or soft.'

'Does God tempt us?' asked Sarah.

'Definitely not. He doesn't want us to do wrong. But someone else does! Who's that?'

'The devil,' replied Sarah. 'But if God doesn't tempt us, why do we ask God not to lead us into temptation?'

'We're asking God to help us to be strong enough to overcome temptation. We're also asking God to help us not to put ourselves in places where we'll be tempted too much.'

'What do you mean, Dad?'

'Well, Paul, suppose some of your friends at school joined a gang of other boys who always got into trouble. You would need God's help not to join the gang, because it's not easy to say no to your friends, even when they do things that are wrong.'

Mr MacDonald could see that Sarah and Paul were beginning to understand. 'I expect you find it a temptation to cheat at school sometimes, don't you?'

Paul and Sarah nodded.

'When we pray, "Lead us not into temptation, but deliver us from evil", we're asking God to help us to do the things which will

61

mean we won't want to cheat, such as doing our work well and not forgetting to do homework. "Deliver us from evil" really explains "Lead us not into temptation". Every day we'll be tempted in some way or other - and often by the devil - and we need God's help to say no to wrong things and yes to right things.'

'Are you tempted then, Dad?' Sarah asked with surprise. 'I didn't think grown-ups were tempted as much as we are.'

Mr MacDonald smiled. 'Yes, I'm often tempted, Sarah. My temptations may be different from yours; but they're very real as well. Each day they come and that's why we need to pray this prayer every day. Temptation can come suddenly and when we least expect it, just as it did for the apostle Peter after the Lord Jesus had been betrayed. Do you remember?'

'Do you mean when he was in the courtyard?'

'Yes, the Lord Jesus was being asked questions by the high priest and Peter was in the courtyard waiting and watching. One of the servant girls of the high priest said, "You were with Jesus, weren't you?" '

'Peter said he wasn't, didn't he?'

'Yes, Paul. Peter was afraid of what was

going to happen to the Lord Jesus and to himself, and he was tempted to pretend that he didn't know the Lord Jesus - and he gave in to the temptation and said to the girl, "No, I wasn't. I don't know what you're talking about." Satan often tempts me to say nothing about the Lord Jesus when I should tell others about Him. When I pray this part of the prayer, I'm telling God I want Him to help me to be ready to speak about the Lord Jesus and not to give in to Satan.'

'What shall we draw tonight?' asked Paul.

'Why not draw Achan hiding his treasure or Peter warming himself by the fire, talking to the servant girl?' answered Mr MacDonald. 'Underneath write -

"We are often tempted."

"We are not strong enough on our own to win against temptation."

"God can make us strong." '

9 Finishing the Scrapbooks

Paul and Sarah were turning over the pages of their scrapbooks.

'It's been fun doing this, hasn't it, Sarah?' Paul said.

'Yes,' Sarah replied. 'I wonder if there's something like it that we can do afterwards. We'll come to the end of The Lord's Prayer tonight. I told Miss Leonard last Sunday what we had been doing each evening with Dad. She said she would like to see my scrapbook when it's done, and she would show it to the rest of the Sunday School class.'

'Perhaps Dad will talk to us about something else when we've finished. Let's ask him, shall we?'

Before Sarah could answer, Mr MacDonald had come in. He heard Paul's question. 'And what are you going to ask me, then? Not to give you any pocket money this week?'

'Not that!' said Paul. 'No, we wondered if you would talk to us about something else from the Bible after we've finished The Lord's Prayer.'

'I expect that can be arranged,' replied Mr

MacDonald with a laugh. 'But let's finish what we're doing first. What's the last part of The Lord's Prayer, Sarah?'

' "For Thine is the kingdom, and the power, and the glory, for ever. Amen.",' answered Sarah.

'That's not really a prayer, is it?' asked Paul. 'It's not asking God for anything, but saying something about God.'

'You're quite right,' said Mr MacDonald. 'This last part of the prayer reminds us that we shouldn't only ask God for things, but also thank Him for what He's given us and praise Him. Let's make sure you understand these words "Thine is the kingdom". What does that mean, Sarah?'

'That God is King and rules over people,' Sarah answered.

Mr MacDonald nodded. 'Yes, that God rules and reigns over everything. It's more important to obey Him than anyone else. That doesn't mean that we don't obey other people and respect them. Some people tried to get the Lord Jesus to say the wrong thing about the Roman emperor Caesar once. They said, "Teacher, we know that you're honest and teach the truth no matter what the consequences.

Now tell us, is it right to pay taxes to the Roman government or not?" But the Lord Jesus knew they were trying to trip Him up, and He said, "Show me the money you use to pay the tax." And they brought Him a coin. And the Lord Jesus said to them, "Whose head is this on the coins?" And they said, "Caesar's." He said to them, "Give to Caesar what belongs to Caesar and give to God what belongs to Him." '

'That was a good answer,' Sarah said.

Mr MacDonald agreed. 'Kings and queens, prime ministers and presidents rule over the countries of the world, but always remember that God's the King of them all.'

'But what happens if the leaders or rulers tell us to do something that God doesn't want us to do?' asked Paul.

'Well, fortunately, that kind of thing doesn't happen often, Paul,' answered Mr MacDonald. 'But when it does, then it's right to obey God, even if it gets us into trouble. Two of the apostles - Peter and John - were arrested for speaking about the Lord Jesus. The rulers in Jerusalem said to them, "You mustn't speak any more about the Lord Jesus. We warn you: if you do, there'll be trouble." Was it right for the rulers to say that?'

'No,' said Paul. 'What did Peter and John say?'

'They said, "We must obey God rather than men." Now, what does "Thine...is the power" mean?'

Paul thought he knew. 'It means that God can do anything.'

'Tell me things God can do that we can't.'

Sarah answered first. 'He can make things from nothing.'

'He can raise people from the dead - like when Jesus raised Lazarus,' added Paul.

'Good,' said Mr MacDonald. 'If God can do these things - and He can - then we know He can answer our prayers too. Now what about "Thine...is the glory"? That isn't so easy for you!'

'Does "glory" mean "praise," Dad?' Sarah asked.

'Yes,' answered Mr MacDonald. 'It means that the Person to be praised for everything that's good is God. When we see our meals ready for us we've Mum to thank, of course, for cooking them; but it's God we especially thank when we have our meals because we know that He made the things we eat and He gives me the health to go to work to earn the money to buy the food.'

Mr MacDonald stopped and thought for a moment. 'Paul, supposing you were tempted to do something wrong. You suddenly remembered that God would help you if you prayed to Him, and you did. What would you say to someone if they said, "That was good of you not to do that wrong thing"?'

'I'd say, "God helped me not to do it," I suppose and that He should be praised, and not me,' answered Paul.

'That's what we mean when we say, "Thine is...the glory". Always remember that when God helps us and answers our prayer we should be quick to say, "Thank you" to Him and to praise Him. Well, I think we've come to the end of the prayer now.'

'We haven't!' said Sarah. 'We haven't spoken about the words "for ever. Amen." '

'Sorry,' said Mr MacDonald. 'God isn't like a human ruler, someone who's great and then one day dies. He lives forever and so His power lasts forever too. We'll never need to stop praising Him.'

'But what about "Amen"?' asked Sarah. 'I've often wondered what it means. Does it mean "the end"?'

'No, it doesn't,' said Mr MacDonald with a smile. 'It means "yes, definitely so." When we've asked God to do something we know will please Him, we say "Amen" to show that we believe that He will answer. It means "It will be so." When we say, "Amen", it's like saying, "Yes, I really mean it." '

'What about when we say "Amen" after someone else has prayed - like in church?' Paul said.

'When we pray together and say "Amen" to the prayer that another person has prayed, we're saying, "Yes, that's my prayer too." So always say "Amen" very clearly after a prayer to show that you mean what has been prayed. Now that really is the end! What are you going to draw?'

'I think I'll draw Jesus holding up the coin with Caesar's head on it and all the people listening to Him,' said Sarah.

'I think I'll draw Peter and John standing in front of the rulers. I'll make the rulers' faces look very cross,' said Paul.

'All right,' said Mr MacDonald. 'And underneath write -

"God is King."

"He can do anything."

"He is to be praised." '

'I want to take my scrapbook to church when I've finished,' said Sarah. 'Miss Leonard wants to see it.'

'Make sure you've completed everything first, then,' said Mr MacDonald. 'I'll bring home a surprise if the books are done well.'

'Oh, good! What will it be?' asked Paul.

'Wait and see! It won't be a surprise if I tell you!'

Bibletime Books

Carine Mackenzie

Story of various Bible characters retold accurately from the Bible. A lively interesting text combined with beautifully illustrated pictures.

Old Testament Characters

Esther	-	The Brave Queen
Gideon	-	Soldier of God
Hannah	-	The Mother who Prayed
Joshua	-	The Brave Leader
Rebekah	-	The Mother of Twins
Ruth	-	The Harvest Girl
also		
Nehemiah	-	God's builder (by Neil Ross)

New Testament Characters

John	-	The Baptist
Mary	-	Mother of Jesus
Peter	-	The Apostle
Peter	-	The Fisherman
Simon Peter-		The Disciple

Coming in 1990

Jonah - The Runaway Preacher
Martha and Mary - Friends of Jesus
32pp

Learn About God

Carine Mackenzie

Eight books for pre-school age on the character of God.
Full colour pictures throughout with minimum of text.

God Has Power

God Answers Prayer

God Knows Everything

God Is Kind

God Is Faithful

God Is Everywhere

God Made Everything

God Never Changes

16pp

The
High Hill

Pauline Lewis

Biblical novel set in the time of Elijah with its central event being the encounter between Elijah and the prophets of Baal on Mt. Carmel. The story is about Nathan and Anna who know that one day they will be married since it has been arranged by their respective parents.

Read how their faith in God is tested in these stirring times.

for 10-15 years

80pp   *pocket paperback*

The White Stone

Pauline Lewis

Biblical novel set in the time of Solomon.

Michael's father is unwell and in danger of losing his property. Yet at one time he was a friend of the young prince, Solomon: even saving his life.

Read how Michael diligently tries to gain access to Solomon's palace and how the wise king deals with the problem.

for 10-15 years

80pp   *pocket paperback*

A
Different Mary

Anne Rayment

Christian novel based on a character called Mary.

She is thirteen, from a broken home, rejected by her mother. However she meets the Fellows family and their friends at Gladstone Street Baptist Church.

A very topical story, well written and easy to read.

For 10-14 year old girls.

196pp   *large paperback*

Only Children

Anne Rayment

Joey has problems as a fourteen year old Christian.

His parents have divorced and his father remarried.

Joey stays with his mum but idolizes his father who invites him to stay for a while.

Joey is fond of Camilla, who belongs to a strange cult.

Then Emma, a school friend, disappears after being befriended by Camilla.

How does Joey and his sister, Sarah, aged twelve, react to all this? What about Sophie, a Christian the same age as Joey?

for 11-15 years

128pp   *pocket paperback*